# DREAM WEAVERS

Edited by

Rebecca Mee

First published in Great Britain in 2001 by
*POETRY NOW*
Remus House,
Coltsfoot Drive,
Peterborough, PE2 9JX
Telephone (01733) 898101
Fax (01733) 313524

*Copyright Contributors 2001*

HB ISBN 0 75432 662 4
SB ISBN 0 75432 663 2

# FOREWORD

Although we are a nation of poets we are accused of not reading poetry, or buying poetry books. After many years of listening to the incessant gripes of poetry publishers, I can only assume that the books they publish, in general, are books that most people do not want to read.

Poetry should not be obscure, introverted, and as cryptic as a crossword puzzle: it is the poet's duty to reach out and embrace the world.

The world owes the poet nothing and we should not be expected to dig and delve into a rambling discourse searching for some inner meaning.

The reason we write poetry (and almost all of us do) is because we want to communicate: an ideal; an idea; or a specific feeling. Poetry is as essential in communication, as a letter; a radio; a telephone, and the main criterion for selecting the poems in this anthology is very simple: they communicate.

# CONTENTS

## AMOEBA ISLANDS

A girl dreams of islands,
jungle green, circled
with suntan strips of sand.
She creates their shape, their structure,
amoebas in an azure paper sea.
She draws contours,
fingerprints mountains, valleys, forests,
slices them, like a ripe mango,
into sections,
building them up again
from another angle,
another dimension of their beauty,
their geography of raindrops
livid as lava, mottled skin
of snakes sloughed upon the shore.

She breathes in ink blots, chalk dust,
rain on glass.

*Sue Chadd*

## FIGHT OR FLIGHT

Light led Newman
safely through the storm
on the boat tossed by the elements
inspiring him to pray 'Lead Kindly Light'.

Tongues, thousands of them,
sing to Wesley's hymns
now as then
only fewer these days
nothing could contain them.

That light illuminates you and me
for, if we are burning with it
like Newman and Wesley,
it can do nothing but shine.

*Robert D Shooter*

## THE ISLAND

Mine is an island
of secrets -
of half-hidden coves,
massaged
by Neptune's warm fingers,
where rhinestone rock pools,
cradle baby crabs.

- of postcard cottages,
nursed
in the womb of Mother Earth.

- of buried fossils,
fingerprints from
lost aeons of time,
entombed
in ancient strata.

Mine is an island gem,
an emerald
sewn on the hem
of England's skirt,
where villas
of ruined Rome,
rub shoulders
with Great Victoria's home -
and sunsets burn,
where smugglers' tide
is turning gold.

*Jennifer D Wootton*

## AND NATURE SMILED

In my Druid days, when native plants
Were nibbled, and earth's brown blood
Gurgled in the stream, and river banks
Were strewn with the tribe,
Late cool evenings warmed to the
Sound of crackling, and the smell of
Earth seeped from the hissing
Bark of roasting sapwood.

There, tentative fingers stimulated flesh
And innocence prepared itself,
To allow the foraging.

How deep the cave of wishing;
How shallow the pool of conquest.
We took more than the scent of earth
Home to our caves, in those far-off days,
When nature smiled, concealing her knowledge
And approval of our ways.

*Alex Laird*

## DALE ABBEY
## MY PLACE OF DREAMS

No worries lie
Over there
Beyond,
All that I've faced today.
An oasis of green
Full of life, everywhere.
Softly rising, from hill to hill.
Silhouetted,
Stands the mill,
Turning all that's bad, into good.
There,
Cattle graze
In sunlit haze;
Like me,
Chewing things over
And making rainbows
From storm filled skies.

*Pam Summers*

## IN THE DREAM FIELD

Out here we are summer
Slated and caned
Near mentally deranged
With wine covered sunshine

Out here we are the season of love
Bush gifts from above
Head honey from the Gods
Knives on the stove

Out here in panorama
Music feels like the air
Fortunes of war
Are built far from here

Out here we are ivy climbing
In vessels of free spirits
Vassals of friends
Out here this immortal
Is loved and amazed

*Anora Kay*

## CASA DOS SONHOS - HOUSE OF DREAMS

At last we came upon it
down a dusty track, right at the very end,
sitting there midst the orange groves,
quietly nestling
in the Portuguese countryside.
Gates open to welcome us
Casa dos Sonhos - House of Dreams.

The keys are under the black dog -
and so they are!
We wrestle with the unfamiliar lock
and enter; cool and dim, clay tiled floors,
white walls.
The house enfolds us.
Blue and white flowered curtains
move minimally in the whispering wind.
the window frames the Mediterranean scene
of starkly coloured shrubs 'gainst
flowering fronds of green
and dusky mountains afar in gently graded greys.
Morning glory swirls brashly round the telegraph pole
purple trumpets proud against the azure blue
of the sky.
Up the steps and through the gate
the pool sparkles and awaits;
pink climbing shrubs in terracotta pots
'neath cooling bamboo shade.
The sounds are of the birds, the wind and the bees,
A house of dreams indeed.
The peace and quiet is soothing balm to the soul
to reduce the toll
that busy life at home puts on us all.
For this short time -
we'll dream along with you.

*Marjorie Haddon*

## IN MY DREAMS

When I awoke this morning,
    I looked at the clear blue sky.
I remembered that last lovely holiday
    We shared together - you and I.

As we went on our way to the airport
    The puddles were full, and it was raining fast.
It was so dull and miserable
    We wondered how long it would last.

It was cloudy and dull, when we arrived in Jersey,
    But the sun quickly broke through
And shone all day, taking the dark clouds away.
Oh how those happy hours flew.

In the hot sunshine we toured the island.
    We were thrilled as we went on our way.
The bright blue sky met the calm blue sea
    As it rolled lazily into the bays.

The Jersey cows, with coats shining like satin
    Watched as we passed them by.
On elegant arched necks they moved their heads
    And followed us with inquisitive eyes.

We visited the German Bunkers.
    Our imagination was put to the test.
How cold in that underground hospital,
    We certainly didn't want to be a guest.

A visit to the pearl and gold factories.
    A pose by Bergerac's car.
The island's breathtaking scenery.
    The night skies covered in stars.

Is there another island so beautiful
    With its beaches, castles and Napoleon Towers?
A zoo to breed endangered species.
    I could go on for hours and hours.

Some day I must go back to the island,
    This time it will be on my own.
In my imagination you will be with me there
    I certainly won't be alone.

***Joan Smith***

## ZA ZORX

Have you been to Za Zorx?
It's a place of fantasy dreams.
I have been there myself,
In a cellar of death, I hear your screams!

Za Zorx knows your madness,
I would love to love, love to love me!
Or something non-resistant
Like a drink of fresh insanity!

Have you been to Za Zorx?
It is where your mind warps.
If you stay in Za Zorx
You could end up a corpse!

Za Zorx has no owner,
But he is someone quaint!
Your digital circuits are corroding,
And you need a new coat of paint!

The monumental Za Zorx
It has loving as a dead metal brain!
If you're in need of a good sedative . . .
Za Zorx will take away your pain!

*Peter Steele*

## UNTITLED

I remember when.
Worn out shoes, scratched up knees
A jumper threadbare, stiff in cuff
From umpteen usage for nose and such.
The bite of strap from teacher's strict
Red weal's of discipline in its grip.
Rupert Bear in daily paper
Teaching of a different nature.
Open fields and hills to roam
Safe to let loose on your own.
Following the baker's horse
Garden manure not to be lost.
Cart load of coal dumped in the street
Stacked in backyard before you eat,
Pit clothes soaking in tin bath
After Ma had washed dad's back,
Stale jam sandwich returned from pit
Eaten with great pride
A penny for the pictures
Which were all black and white,
Cleaning fire range with black lead
A must also the front door step.
Queued five hours for bread and meat
Dropped under a bus
Took home in fright now tyred to mush.
Sweets were rationed a quarter a week
But I still have all my front teeth.
A bonfire large to celebrate
Returning heroes from the war,
In shadowy fringe I kissed and touched
Young Jenny I adored.

*R Fallon*

## UNTITLED

Gentle night with darkness profound
In swirls of black velvet wrap me around
Let me close my eyes in pure serene bliss
And may Heaven bless me this night with a kiss

*Barbara Robson*

## YESTERDAY'S COCOON

To trace the path that once we walked,
The dreams we dreamed, the way we talked.
To re-live once more those twilight years,
Yet never know the pain, the tears.
That little house where first we dwelt,
My mind's eye conjures all we felt.
Just you and I in our own cocoon,
A vision in today's new moon.
That same moon that shone so long ago
Before our lives collided so.

*M A Shipp Yule*

## LOVER'S WOOD

The roses bloom along the way
A thousand violins seem to softly play
Cascades of water splash the air
And rainbows seem to gather there

The cool night breezes cool the skin
And gentle deer go wanderin'
The flowers hide their heads in sleep
And through them we do softly creep

We see a cross within the wood
A place to kiss as lovers should
We stop awhile to shed a tear
A broken heart lies buried there

The grass is green and soft, not torn asunder
Inviting us to stop and wonder
Who the architect could be
And was it meant for you and me

The smell, the colours, quite suffice
We could have been in Paradise
For love is pure and knows no fear
No evil spirits linger here

The stars in iridescent flight
So far away but still in sight
Throughout the night we see some fall
Like candles lighting Heaven's hall

The trees form steeples of lofty boughs
Like the church where we made our wedding vows
The moon is a jewel
Set in the deep black sea of devotion
The sight of which stirs lovers
And fills them with emotion
The smell of jasmine, rose and pine
'Twas a night like this I made you mine

The creatures of the night do play
And a nightingale sings its heart away
The gentle rain that falls in shower
Afraid to show its awesome power
It falls on hair and cheek and breast
A wet caress from Nature's chest

The streams where water runs and surges
The fish that succumb to its urges
They feel the clear cool water's kiss
Then vanish in the morning mist

When love is lost and then re-won
We know we're not the only one
Love sometimes goes in fits and starts
The corridor of time is paved
With countless broken hearts

Your kiss is sweet, your mouth divine
Your lips taste like a summer wine
I say no more, your praises sung
Like angels weeping on my tongue

Oh gods of trees, Oh gods of air
Have pity on the one's who dare
To tread amongst your realms for free
And revel in your majesty.

*James V Sullivan*

# MOONLIGHT ON THE TREES

The moonlit road was long and straight
Trees on its edges glistened white,
Leaves dancing in the gusting wind
Twisting like dancers in the night.

The road was old, walked over forever
By the marching boots of Caesar armies.
Tramping to battle vain and glorious
Sometimes returning battered and broken.

When the moon rides high in a windy sky
And the trees on the roadside quiver
You can sense the tramp of ghostly feet
Echoing along the years with solemn tread.

Row upon row, line on line, shoulder to shoulder
They moved in silent order shining bravely.
With helmets casting their faces in shadow
Spears glittering in shafts of moonlight.

As the moon settles quietly behind the hills
Darkness slides back once again in command
The marching soldiers in silence fade away
And the road sighs in its loneliness.

*E W Branagan*

## OLD PHOTOGRAPHS

These faded photos that I hold
are many lifetimes spent.
I only know what I've been told . . .
No voice, no sound, no feel, no scent.

Graceful girls with braided hair.
Flower-decked hats that never fade.
Khaki-clad men, I shed a tear
For soldiers and the price they paid.

They look at me. They have no speech.
What were their joys and fears?
Did they have hopes beyond their reach?
What kept them going through the years?

Sweetness of child wonder:
Bunches of wild flowers:
Long gone days of summer,
They have their secrets.
We have ours.

*Isobel G King*

## MY SECRET PLACE

There is a secret place where I can dream
Where peace and love reign supreme
This place is deep within my mind
A place that only God can find
A place where all problems disappear
And passed loved ones are never near
A place where there are gardens fair
And sounds of nature fill the air
There is a warm and gentle breeze
Where bluebells sway beneath the trees
Little streams go trickling by
And sunbeams dance beneath the sky
My secret place is full of magic
Where all is life and nothing's static
A place where spring is always there
And winter storms would never dare
My secret place is a world apart
Where reality ends and daydreams start
And as I wander over hills and dales
Past crystal fountains and sunlit vales
I finally reach the rainbow's end
And there I find a hand outstretched by a friend

*Sylvia Gwilt*

## RIDING THE CLOUDS

We stepped upon a carpet
and glided through the air,
into a fairyland of dreams
a wonderland - a fair.
Where angels serenaded us
with joyous tunes on harps -
we danced upon the cotton clouds
walked a crooked path.

The hedgerows shone with golden pearls -
every rich man's prayer -
but at the rainbow's edge there lurked -
the great black witch's claw.
Our light was deemed to fade,
for dragons, demons came -
we didn't have our magic wands
and danced into the flames.

Then suddenly a knight on horse -
came galloping our way.
He challenged them - a duel was fought
and all would be okay.
When the fighting ceased to exist
we were beckoned to his castle -
greeted by his queen to dine
then lived there ever after.

*Wendy Watkin*

## WATERVILLE

There's a place that's deep in my heart
A place forever on my mind
It's the quaintest little village
You could ever hope to find
It nestles in the green fields of Ireland
It's a place called Waterville
And deep in my memory it has a place still
The village where I was born and raised
Working while the cattle grazed
A lovely quiet farm
Surrounded by mountains and lakes
So tranquil and so calm
My memories of lazy childhood hours
Walking the mountain tracks
By fields full of shamrock and heather flower
Fishing and cycling down the lanes
Riding up by the cross home to tarmons again
That lovely place remains in my heart
I know it always will
My beautiful homeland Ireland
And my village of Waterville.

*Trudie Sullivan*

## LITTLE GREEN MEN

We live a life of dreams
Of starlight and moonbeams
Where our sleepy minds will take us
No one knows
So-called visits in the nights
Of aliens making epic flights
I'm talking of elusive UFOs
My mind can't contemplate
That distances so great
Will put a living ET on our shores
A space flight nightly hop
Like a visit to the corner shop
After all it's just four light years
Down the road
If it's true what the tabloids pen
Of their visits now and then
Surely it's us earthlings
Who must be the little green men

*Brian Wardle*

## THE MEADOW SO BEAUTIFUL

The meadow so beautiful,
The grass so green,
The trees rustling in the soft breeze,
The cows drinking water,
From the stream.

All is quiet,
Not a stir,
Just the sounds of nature,
Everywhere,
For us to share.

*Jane Milthorp*

## NATURE'S SPACES, THE SACRED PLACES

Encounters of summer wonder, found now wherever
the hawthorn blushes from deep pink to red, and the usual
white snow like ladened blossom.
The scent of flowers and grass, the whistles and calls, songs of
birds filling bright days.
In deepening summer nights on the verge of sleep . . . and sweet
sunny dreams, look up among the myriad stars, a half-moon
rise comes, writes across the skies dark page of night.
Moonlight reflecting sun spirit force, onto this turning,
world below, as it spins people into dreams.
Here in the wake of summer's moon, on the drift of
dancing dark and light, we surrender to dreaming night . . .
Then wake and see where, the fields fill yellow gold,
custard, with bright buttercups!
In the sunlight, nature's colours - the sacred places,
reflect from sunny smiles and happy faces . . .
Where the wild flowers of summer's colours, of alpine
blues and scarlet poppies, hedgerows of
wild roses, woodland flowers scatter all around, unfurling
ferns and purple heathers, daisies abound -
at every turn, beauty emerging out of the sun
dappled greens . . .
My soul dances in these colours, plays in the breeze,
finds wonder in nature's bounty, beauty and peace
among the living trees.

*Paul Holland*

## AT ONE WITH THE WORLD

Tropical dummer boy
Bananas, mangroves
Catching lobster sized crayfish
Beating out old grooves

At night singing
Monkeys up above
Crickets play on ancient song
Mapping out the stars

Flamingos at dawn
Journey of vision
Gazing at the world beneath
Where first man once stood

*Rodger Moir*

# NEW YORK

I'd like to visit America,
New York would be my choice
I'd stroll along to Central Park
and listen to the voices
of the people passing by,
and then I'd just sit back,
relax and watch the stars shine
in the night sky.

I'd take a famous yellow cab
to see the famous sights
and watch the city that never sleeps
shine in the bright lights.

I'd like to see a Broadway show
see Times Square and 42nd Street
and then visit the City stores
and buy myself a treat.

They call it the Big Apple
and when you visit you'll
see why they do, because to
visit New York would be
a dream come true.

*Lorraine Dignen*

## NOW IS ALWAYS

What is the 'I' of 'me'?
With my eye I see
But external objects
Hinder free-seeing
Of inner soul and spirit and being.

From moment to moment I am becoming
Living in time and space, 'I am' something.
Can you remember
The moment you came from?
Can you interpret
The past experience
Which lives in the 'now' of present action?

Take the living moment
And experience the experience
Of being a being of light and life,
An aware and awake continuum,
An external breath, permanent yet brief.

*David W Hill*

## SEARCHING

I dig deep into
Recesses of my mind
Looking for a spark;
Blowing for ignition.

My creative instincts
Were too long on hold;
Too long unproductive.
I need proof of life.

But, the tools lay idle
On the table; paper
Remained unused.
I could find no start.

Then finally, having
Suffered and sulked,
The words-so-shy-creep
Forth, furtively, into a sense.

***Colm Hannon***

## HAWAII

My place of dreams
I dream one day to go to Hawaii
Hot, sunny, heavenly delight
I've seen Hawaii on television
I dreamt about going
I've been in my dreams
I loved Hawaii Five O
'Book 'em Dano'
I dream that one day
I will get married in Hawaii
What a dream come true
This would be
This heavenly, delightful place
Maybe one day dreams will come true
I hope this one does
Me, Michelle, in Hawaii
A place of my dreams
I hope so
Hawaii I will go to
Honolulu Hawaii
Dream of the present
Future I will be there
Honolulu Hawaii
I will be coming in the future

*Michelle Knight*

## WARM THOUGHTS

Under the warmth, I lay me down
My limbs become languid and heavy
I relax and let my body turn brown
Factor 20 at the ready!

Up above a palm tree sways
My sun glasses hide my eyes
I'm all alone with the warming rays
I feel the heat start to rise

I drift away to another land
Where I'm floating on a warm sea
Surrounded by shifting silvery sand
No stress, I'm worry free

I close my eyes and hear the sound
Of a boat come chugging by
But I know that no one else is around
Just me and a seagull's cry

Then a worldly sound invades my head
With a click, a spit and a cough
It's the timer on my sun bed
And it's turned the darned thing off!

*Jackie Johnson*

## AS DUSK CRAWLS

Place Millennium,
In village Mogoditshane;
Convenient distance from Gaborone,
Capital of Botswana.

Place Millennium,
Architectural longing,
For original lessons;
A spaceship, restful,
Contemplative.

The western theatre.
Teardrops, touched, by deep pleasure;
The Lord's splendour, indeed, a treasure.

As dusk crawls,
I sit under a mother tree;
Birds, from wanders, free,
Streaming back,
Coming home,
To eternal comfort.

Trees, dipping, ever so passionately,
Into silhouette truth;
Readiness, in journeying,
To worlds, a cleansing, and pamper.

Night falls,
Place Millennium, glows warm;
Up above,
Stars, in all fashion, of fertile life.

The soul,
And the soul, sails;
Where fortune,
Chisels meaning.

*Rowland Warambwa*

# A WORLD OF BOOKS

A library full of books off all descriptions,
  a room full of silence where I can read.
There my imagination can work overtime,
  what more could any man need?
The ideal place for others may be a desert island,
  a paradise in the sun.
Or a cottage in the country surrounded by nature,
  maybe a holiday resort purpose built for fun.
I prefer the quiet life, solitude is my friend,
  the sanctuary of my own company.
Here I can share the thoughts of other writers,
  what greater joy could there be?

*M A Challis*

## TIME AND CHANCE

A race is set before me
Who will run in this race?
The race of life I say
The race is not to the swift
That's what I hear
Nor the battle to the strong
Neither yet bread to the wise
Nor yet riches to men of understanding
Nor yet favour to men of skill
But time and chance
Happens to them all
In the race of life
Man also knows not
His times as the fishes
That are taken in an evil net
And as the birds that are
Caught in the snare
So are the ones of men
Snared in an evil time
When it falls suddenly upon them
Then! This race is for all
Now I understand the rules
Before I begin the race
Set before me
I ask for Grace to finish.

*Ebenezer Essuman*

## UNCONDITIONAL LOVE

I sit on the beach
Enjoying the peace and tranquillity.
Feeling your embrace, I can forget about my day.
Relaxing, taking in your mood
Your waves breathe in and out like a heart beat.
In the distance you allow boats to glide gently over you.
The sun beats down, reflecting different shadows across you.
Clouds look like balls of cotton wool.
I sit and ponder, I could be anywhere in the world.
With hot sun, blue skies, yellow sands, and clear blue sea,
The beach is not decked out with sun beds or cluttered with people
But is beautiful and peaceful.
The silence is broken now and again by the screeching of gulls
Or the sound of your waves crashing onto the rocks.
All around it's breath-taking.
But each day I come here you never look the same,
So many changes but you're still able to maintain your elegance
and beauty.
I feel your energies as you push to the shore.
Clouds take different shapes across the sky.
Your sunset creates a different scene.
As darkness falls I leave you behind
But like a love affair, I could never give you up.
I look forward to seeing you tomorrow.
Not knowing your mood.

*Angie*

## DREAMS

What are dreams?
It's something that we think,
Something that we wish.
It doesn't mean a thing to anyone else.
Good or bad, happy or sad,
We dream them in our sleep.

They seem so real,
We are all there playing parts,
Mothers, fathers, friends and lovers.
They are things that may happen in the day,
Or just before we sleep.
They seem to come to life in our dreams,
Oh, so sweet, yet oh, so frightening.

We toss and turn all night long,
To wake for just a while,
And then it's back to sleep again,
To dream until the dawn.

At last the morning comes,
To wake us from these things,
We take a while to come round, to think,
Was it real, or was it just a *dream?*

***Sue Hutchings***

## WHERE THE VEIL IS THIN

I'm captive to black
bound by city-suit and tie
I commute in the dark
and feel the joy in me die

I survive
behind the mask I wear
until I come alive

where western isles lay bare
their colours
too true for surprise
and the shadows drop from my eyes

where a fanfare of red slips into the sea
and ribbons of light trail scarlet and gold
through a turquoise sky reluctant to fade
and luminous hours soothing as ether
fold me in sapphire and jade

where cuckoo and lark continue to sing
under stars that cling to incipient dark

where the veil is thin
between me and heaven.

*Angela Butler*

## DREAM A DREAM

A place of dreams should live within
your heart, your soul and mind
however you behold in sight
a judgement that is blind . . .

Lift up your thoughts and mediate
think on in happy frame
a dormant dream waits to be stirred
to lapse it is to maim . . .

You ponder how to dream a dream
it's so easy to perform
to dream and wonder when you wish
can ride you through a storm . . .

So dream your dream and sing a song
from thoughts within your heart
travel; far and see the world
dreaming dreams is quite an art!

*Margarette L Damsell*

## MUSIC OF MEMORIES

I have walked from the shadows
To walk the shore by the sea,
Here memories flood back to me,
Of sunset isles and treasured smiles.

So long I watch the breaking waves,
Swirling, rippling, smoothing sandy shores,
Shoes and socks I cast aside,
Now with bare feet I meet the tide.

The seagulls call mocking from flight
Smooth, soft feathers grey and white,
The far horizon also mocks my thoughts,
From across the sea comes smiles to me.

Gentle soft music - recalling musical memories,
The loves I've found and lost,
Music we played and loved to share
I recall those friends so far away.

Now with music and those smiles,
I can see and hear a congregation,
Music played for friends - delayed,
All recalled by musical memories.

***Des Lamb***

## DREAM GARDENS

Gardens of magic, gardens of dreams,
Gardens visited by rippling streams.
Somewhere where water runs over your toes
And invites you to follow wherever it goes.
Gardens of beauty where unicorns meet
And squirrels come looking for something to eat.
Cascading waterfalls to refresh the sight,
Sparkling diamonds - reflections of light.
Dragonflies meet at the start of the day,
Mischievous butterflies kiss them away.
In rainbow colours a joy to behold,
Nature's true gifts more precious than gold.
Sensual gardens to captivate me,
When I need to escape that's where I'll be.
Embracing the freedom I feel all around,
Lost in the wonder of mystical sound.
Gardens of magic, gardens of dreams,
Where unicorn babies play with moonbeams.
Somewhere where problems can all fade away
And time can stand still for a very long stay.
If you'd care to visit then first free your mind
And leave all your baggage and soon you will find,
That gardens of magic and rapturous bliss
Are yours when you enter on the wings of a wish.

*Denny*

## EVENING ON THE CANAL

The evening comes
Shows something seen and thought
Of beauty.
The clouds fleece through
The clearing evening sky.
May flies are dancing
In the long grasses.
A slight breeze cools my brow
And ripples flowing waters
Gently through
Where we are moored.
And all around,
The idyllic English countryside.
A yellow light shines within the boat
And faintly can be heard
The boiling kettle.
The scene like pages of a turning book
The story yet untold.
The light finally fades
And into the boat I descend
The day remembered.

*C J Bayless*

## HORSE POWER

I climbed aboard this pure white horse,
Speeding off into the night,
Together we jumped hedges and trees,
We ran so far and fast,
We caught up with the morning light,

Up glass mountains with clouded tops,
Down into valleys of cardboard boxes and road cones,
Forests of matchsticks were burning bright,
Marshmallows houses of blue and red,
Were placed in clusters around demilitarised zones,

Battlefields were littered with death and destruction,
Preserved as a warning to man, deep in the mists of time,
A distant bell tolled, as a shooting star caught my eye,
Liquorice trees produced jelly bean fruit,
Birds sang happily from trees of orange and lime,

We jumped a rainbow, landed in the eye of a storm,
Lightning forked the clouded sky,
Deep rooted trees fell at our feet,
Forming a road down which we made our escape,
To a market in old Baghdad, where greedy slavers their trade did ply.

We crossed the sea with one huge bound,
To a land of castles, princesses and kings,
Beyond the castles keep, darkness and evil lurked,
Disguised as traffic wardens, and white knights,
But none could restrain me and my steed with wings,

Suddenly I hear a voice thanking us for travelling on Virgin trains,
And that this train will terminate at Bournemouth Central because
of leaves on the track,

My beautiful white charger stops, bucks and rears tipping me
from the saddle.
I feel myself tumbling through space, my horse disappeared
into the buffet car,
A tall uniformed man says tickets please sir, oh and welcome back.

*P J Littlefield*

## DOING NOTHING!

Sitting doing nothing?
No! Not really so
I sit and see, the clear fresh clouds
In early morning glow
Overhead the birds arise
And sing their joyous song
Down below, a cricket chirps
All nature joins along
And in the hush of morning, all things are as one
A sudden move, and all too soon, the pleasant scene has gone
It takes a quite, reflective mood
To take in nature's plan
The spring that comes so fresh and new
As when time began

*Gladys Mary Gayler*

## A PLACE OF DREAMS

Can be within the night
Resting on your pillow,
Many visual sights,
The mind's eye sees,
Vast memories,
Of a favourite scene
Of peace so serene,
This place for me, is perched on a rock,
High above a blue lagoon,
Surrounded by trees,
A cathedral of stone
With a beautiful dome,
Making one respect
Our fore fathers intellect.
Once inside tranquillity reigns
One can act quite sane,
The world outside don't exist,
You have nothing to resist,
Only time will consume
That visual theme,
When daylight arrives
And devour your dream

*Barbara R Lockwood*

## I'LL TAKE THE RIGHT . . .

My door into the outside world
has two ways that I can go.
To the left's all hustle and bustle,
to the right everything slow.
Sometimes I do not have a choice,
to the left I tread my way.
When the choice is mine I take a right
into my garden and there to stay.
To sit amidst the roses,
watch the busy bees kiss every one.
I have a lawn upon which to wander
as the stress is all undone.
I forget about the left side,
always prefer the right.
There lies my peace and happiness,
'tis a lazy, slow delight.
When I spend time in the garden
I enjoy everything in view.
To the left it's all material,
mostly fake, just not much true.

*Rosie Hues*

## A PLACE OF DREAMS

I guard it well, my place of dreams,
For there I meet with you,
No other place is possible,
For you cannot come true!

The place we meet is dear to me,
Its beauty beyond wonder,
The music there our song of joy,
This place, no one may plunder.

Yet, if this dream cannot come true,
No heart shall then be broken,
It gently holds the heart of me,
I need no other token.

*Mary Hughes*

## COME WITH ME

Under the wide branches of the sycamore tree
I sit and ponder the peace and tranquillity,
Here shadows dance and patterns shape the ground
And warm air skim the leaves to touch my face,
This is my secret place, my place of dreams,
I'll take you there, if you would come with me.

We'll walk along the narrow winding footpath,
Where myriad of beautiful wild flowers stand
Silent, bowing to the sun beneath the open sky.
Watch the startled song birds as they soar and fly
Out of sight, over the shrouded hilltops
But listen to the skylark, as it hovers on the wing.

In the deep quiet of the mystic forest
Feel the overwhelming hold of nature's hand,
The surge of its energy calming the soul,
You'll be haunted, enchanted, rooted to the spot
A falling leaf will gently brush your cheek,
The moment will last forever in your imagination.

*Wilma Nicholas*

## THE PROMISED LAND

A quiet, deserted place it is -
The seashore early in the day.
Before the crowds move in en masse
And children laugh and shout at play.

Now, as I stroll a while, and sit
And rest myself upon a rock,
I watch the sunrise silently -
For it is only seven o'clock.

The wonder of God's handiwork
Will never fail to humble me,
As ripples on the shingle creep,
With roaring breakers out to sea.

Sandcastles by the water's edge,
Built by the children yesterday,
Are threatened by the rising tide,
And soon will all be swept away.

My thoughts compare this with our lives,
When all is well - we walk up tall.
But when fate is unkind to us
We may lose our resolve and fall.

Leave far behind life's busy rush
With its frustrations, faults and tears,
Reflect in a secluded place
To lift us up and calm our fears.

The mighty sea, the gentle waves,
Weaving patterns in the sand,
Can take our cares and doubts away,
And lead us to our 'Promised Land'.

*Jim Holmes*

## MY TRANQUIL MORNING

With respect I watch the ocean
and the rolling foaming waves,
where restless waters never still
wash over shipwrecked graves.

I wandered down the track
to the golden sandy bay
and was greeted by noisy gulls
as they swooped and dived at play.

I inhaled the fresh salt air
it blew the cobwebs away,
the warmth from the sun
was a perfect start to the day.

I sat on a rock enjoying the moment
all thoughts of work cast aside
and felt at peace alone
just me and the oncoming tide.

*Linda Beavis*

## FROM MY WINDOW

A view of the sea I see from my chair,
White sails gliding here and there -
One large island - others are small
A valley of pines majestically tall -
Reach down to the yachts
And main shipping lane
With distant hills and ruined castle
All looks calm - not much hassle
Then my eyes look down on the garden again
The green lawn and flowers, blossoms galore -
Real squirrels and birds, false one's too
Two benches to sit on with a view to adore -
Gnomes, bambis, a dog - a stone man on a seat
A bird bath, shells, four plastic geese;
My dream comes true whilst I sit in my chair
As I open my window - for a breath of sea air.

*Constance Heald*

## AT COMMUNION

Bread from grain and wine from grape,
Tokens of our Saviour's love.
These we take for his dear sake,
One His body - one His blood.

When we kneel before His table,
As we've done so oft' before,
We remember his great promise,
'I am with you evermore'.

*Janet Cavill*

## My Willow And I

Neath your shade I come to life,
Free from troubles, worries strife.
No matter when by day or night,
Your beauty fills me with delight.

My arms around your trunk entwine,
To heal once more that heart of mine.
Your strength into my soul will flow,
Peace, tranquillity, at once bestow.

My heart, my mind again be stilled,
My empty bowl once more refilled.
These precious moments with you alone,
All fears, all doubts away have flown.

My existence at once you justify,
The whole of me you satisfy.
My Weeping Willow so tall, so grand,
The real me only you can understand.

*Shula Bailey*

## A SECRET COVE

As I wonder on my travels,
Exploring every corner on my way,
The excitement of what I find,
Reveals treasures hard to say!

Down a long, steep, twisting road,
Through the white sparkling cliffs,
Capped with growth cascading,
Just like a green snow drift.

For as the sea comes crashing in,
Then rebounds off the cliff's face,
Sends the water flying in the air,
Like diamonds floating in outer space!

Warm and cosy in this cove,
Tranquil time just drifts past,
For here was a place undisturbed,
Away from our hectic lives at last!

I've found the beauty of this world,
Which no man could ever buy,
God created all this for us,
So don't spoil it or pass it by!

*Ann Beard*

## FOOL'S PARADISE

'Still living with your parents at 33?'
Like a couch-potato - he sits and does nothing.
Mum's sofa - cushions him from reality.
'Me Tarzan, you Jane - we go swinging.'
Then John's rudely awakened by the 'The toast is burning!'
He's living on a fool's paradise,
Where variety is the spice of life.

Jane ignores the bills and the housing form.
'Oh to win a million or even a few grand
So there's no more treadmill work every morn.'
Jane floats away on a Turkish carpet to a wondrous land
Where an ear-ringed genie bows: 'Your wish is my command.'
She's living on a paradise of fools.
'Dive from that waterfall into the pool.'

Clambering up the beanstalk, Jack was full of beans.
Because of no mortgage, kids or down-to-earth wife,
Jack could indulge in far-fetched dreams.
Is your future rosy in the kingdom of Fife?
Even for Adam and Eve there was trouble and strife.
Thrown out like rotten apples; the same they couldn't face
And they believed their Eden home was a perfect place.

The conflicts were dumped on Botany Bay;
He's unaffected by foot and mouth and blind to war and pain.
Now Australia was their prison until their dying day
If only life was beer and skittles and castles in Spain
Keep searching for the pot of gold after the illusive rain.
If a fool's paradise is sun, sea and smiles,
It's no longer funny on these Silly Isles.

*Mark Young*

## OBERE AND UNTERE

I dreamt hordes stood below - agog -
Ecclesia and sad Synagogue,
And shunned the Bamberg Knight benign,
Of proud, bold Hohenstaufen line.

I dreamt I leapt eight hundred years,
And saw him hewn with sweat and tears,
With French finesse and German grit,
By Norman glass and candle lit.

I dreamt I witnessed grief and gore,
The Bamberg Rider sent to war
To galvanise a Fuhrer's race,
To hang his head in deep disgrace.

I dreamt brave Knight left Meuse and Somme
And graced again the Kaiserdom,
At rest between stark Rhineland choirs,
Symbol of peace 'neath towering spires.

*Peter Davies*

## PLACE OF DREAMS

My paradise is here with you
In our castles in the sky;
Where we can sit and just hold hands
And the clouds, they saunter by.

The azure of the sky dips down
To meet sea of aquamarine;
Leafy branches, fresh and new,
In nature's smartest shades of green.

If we could only stay right here
For ever and a day;
My special place would be so real
And not just a dream away.

*Sandra Benson*

## OF SILENCE

I've long since thought, of how I'd feel
With blues all around, it's so unreal,
Shades of grey, mingled forth, with dawn,
To keep one's self, for there upon,
It isn't come easy, in fact, somewhat hard,
Pushing of dewdrop, along lest regard,
Thereby in patience, its own silly way,
Tomorrow, for yesterday, was that of today,
No meaning whatever, no therefore, at all,
We each have a message, which is to install,
Be ever, so forward, or soonest than said,
It comes here in silence, with nothing instead,
All colour's tone, moreover, shades stay,
To come here and tell us, what's all for delay,
Backwards in something, though not of much now,
There of a sweating, on either, one's brow,
The wrinkled, lined, havings of witness, one fair,
All in amusement, take notes for compare,
Isn't the something, though nothing, at all,
Lines are not dewdropped, that I can recall,
In for a moment, as seconds come near,
Will have with us, happening, an all over sphere,
As global, come warming, it's this so for then,
I've nothing, of any, that I can, say when.

*Hugh Campbell*

## BREATH OF ENGLISH SPRING

The wind whips the coast
and carries sand in undulating wisps.
Across chalk and green it spirals
round and up by the bay in play.

Rape seed plant of yellow, waves
to the breeze, that pushes over land.
Hedgerow waterfalls, with bubble mist
in farmers fields they dip and sip.

The gradient climb gets steeper
and tiny birds bob in rippled breath of tide.
A pair of tiny wings against the wind
with a simple stroke to float.

Down an isle of nature's unlit candles
I like to marry spring.
Where the breeze will blow confetti
with a scented flower shower.

*Maria Bernadette Potter*

# SUMMER CONTEMPLATION

Honeysuckle spread their fingers for the bees
Blue hyacinths nod gently in the breeze.
A blackbird sings its chorus in answer to its mate
Magpies incessant cackling, as on their nests they wait

Lilies stand like soldiers in tightly filled beds
Clematis climbs steadily and intertwine their heads
Baskets swing to and fro in heavy-laden display
Peonies shake their petals free, there's no time to delay

Blue tits fly into their boxes never stopping or to pause
Little ones are waiting with ever-open jaws
Fuchsias are now growing at wonderful speed
Once their flower heads open a profusion will be seen

The long and tiresome winter is now in the past
To sit and bathe in the sun's rays brings a smile that lasts
The summer holds such joy, new life is here to find
In the haven that's my garden contentment rules my mind.

### *Gillian Mullett*

## THAT PLACE

Close your eyes, what can you see?
Can you see the same as me?
Take a trip down memory lane,
Relive that favourite walk again.
I can see that special face!
Bring to mind that lovely place
Over the stile, across the stream,
All I have to do is dream!

*G W Bailey*

## A PLACE IN THE SUN

All my life, I dreamt
I would see, Egypt,
and the River Nile.
The great Sphinx with
its pyramids standing by,
my dreams came true,
tonight I'm here.
A warm, dark night,
not a star in sight
velvet black surrounds me,
I know not what comes next.
But I had not long to wait,
through the dark a voice
is heard, the story has begun.
History over the years,
as each pyramid, secrets
comes, a floodlight circles
its frame, the resting place
of many kings and their queens.
Then comes the turn, of
the Sphinx itself, did
we know, that Cleopatra was
once there, when on the throne she sat.
On his travels, Marco Polo
also passed by, it was all
too much, I closed my
eyes in case my dream,
should break, and I would
not be there.

*Audrey Allen*

# FORGOTTEN DREAMS

to wake from
dreaming into Life
with dreams fulfilled
desires met
to walk the path
first chosen
with you there
not having turned
the silent way
that led to
unfulfilled aloneness in
the nightmare of despair

*Anita Richards*

## MY SPECIAL PLACE

Far, far away from this bustling place
Where everything moves at an alarming pace,
There is a lake, so deep and blue
Surrounded by trees of many a hue.

Early in the morning, I watch the mist rise
Clearing slowly to reveal blue skies.
The sun reflects on the water below
Making it shimmer and softly glow.

Over rugged hills and valleys deep,
Purple heather and wild flowers creep.
Tall trees cast shadows upon the ground,
Animals scurry with rustling sound.

This water so blue and countryside wild
I have dreamed of it since I was a child.
It took half my life for my dream to come true
And I'll always remember, I shared it with you.

*Lynne Walden*

# I BELIEVE IN DREAMS

In my dreams I have a small cottage, with pink roses at the front door,
The curtains are all white and lacy and there's a lovely wooden floor.
Every room is bright and cheery, when I look out I feel so free,
I have bacon butties for breakfast and strawberries and cream for tea.
My kitchen is reasonably large, as I really do love to cook,
But my pride of place is in the lounge, my name upon a book.
For on a shelf up high, for everyone to see,
There sits a book by Jennifer Gleave, written all by me.
One day I will be famous, I feel magic, I just know it,
People will read my book and say, 'Now there's an excellent poet!'
For to have my name in print, is what I've always yearned,
To write astounding poetry, feel good with what I've earned.
This book will be dressed in yellow, my favourite colour of all,
With gold binding entwined throughout it and a purple
ribbon that's small.
The poems will be of a mixture, some funny and some from my life,
The trials and tribulations of being a mother and a wife.
One thing my cottage will have is a view of the beautiful sea,
With lashing blue waves all around it, the sound of tranquillity.
This is my ultimate goal, which could happen later on in my years,
Or perhaps when I'm dead and I'm buried and my children have
cried all their tears.
Until then I'll just keep on waiting, writing about life every day,
Because somebody, somewhere will spot me and then
to me they will say,
'Jennifer, will you write a book, something that you'd
like to get published?'
And the profits will buy me my cottage and my dream will
be finally accomplished.
But for now I will drift off with my dreams, of my book that
is yellow and grand.
And my cottage with sweet lacy curtains, on the beach
that is covered in sand.

*Jennifer Gleave*

## BARBADOS

I love this sea, this Caribbean sea.
Can you take a conch shell and make it into me?
Can I be a hermit, instead of the crab?
To wander through this tired old world
And make it less drab.
Can I be hibiscus, washed upon the shore?
Carried by a wavelet, to float for evermore
Take me to the turtles and throw me in the deep,
Let me climb upon his shell and fake eternal sleep.
Let me be a humming bird alighting on your hand,
Let me fly the night sky, across the coral strand.
Let me leave my senses here upon the sand
And let me be a Bajan until the Promised Land.

*Jennifer H Fox*

## DEAR DIARY

Isn't life strange?
Isn't it though
A question of balance
As far as I know?

A melancholy man
With nowhere to go,
Lost in a lost world,
What's life without hope?

Floating like driftwood
Upon a crystal sea
I came ashore in
A Land Of Make-Believe.

Walking along towards
A house of four doors,
I brought flowers for my lady,
The lady I adore.

Higher and higher
Above 'eternity road'
Watching and waiting
For the people below.

I searched everywhere
But I just couldn't find
The gypsy who said
That she would be mine.

Dear Diary, I wrote
Where on earth could she be
And as the tide rushes in
It was departure for me.

*Brendan G Ryan*

## FORGET THE BOOK

As your eyes broaden
horizons perceived
are very much at your grasp.
In thought you are there in paradise.
guiding golden lights brighten my way
in life and beyond.
Blessed with knowing
space is yours and more.
Have a look
forget the book
act not by line and hook.
The will is for to use to sail.

Mr Caterfly meets Mrs Butterpillar.

Nothing but yesterday
    all for tomorrow
        and evaporation is now.

The seed falls and breaks.
The seed crawls and takes
unravelling destiny as it goes.
Sustaining unto a one-word life,
as vibrations utter.
                    Love.

*Nick Purchase*

## THE JOURNEY OF JOY

Imagine if you will, a perfect place so still
That love is in the very air you breathe.
Where silence is preferred unless love stirs a word,
A noble land that you'd not want to leave.
A meadow in the sun where memories are spun
And wistful thoughts amuse the whole day long.
Everyone acts gently. Everyone is friendly.
Surely this is where your hearts belong.
A perfect place to share, protected by pure prayer
That softens all emotions to a blur.
A home from home, indeed. No heartache, lust or greed.
A haven where God's miracles occur.
Ambitions cast aside. Temptations, too, denied.
Gone are all the traces of Man's strife.
Togetherness and joy for every girl and boy,
For harmony's the purpose of each life.
No demon enters in. This Heaven's without sin.
Each morning brings its glories ever new.
God's clouds all cruise in peace, no storms make them to cease.
The sky remains serene and sapphire blue.
For Jesus rules this land just as His Father planned
And Lucifer is banished to his fate.
God's angels soar above each singing 'God is Love!'
While victory over sin they celebrate.
The Journey of Joy begins with Jesus as your prince -
Subject to the Saviour's Sacred Law,
No purer state than this: salvation, peace and bliss.
Contentment for each soul for evermore.

*D K F Martindale*

## BEHIND CLOSED DOORS

There's a door on the other side of the world,
That no one knocks on anymore,
Come inside and I'll show you what you will find,
To a place where the world has turned a blind eye,
Come inside, where people have left no tears to cry,
Where there's only time and it only flies,
And all you can hear is the whisper of a child,
Only Mother Earth will hold, this pearl in her hand,
The colour of green is in their mind,
Will that green land they ever find?
There's no rain, and there's pain in their hearts,
As they walk no more,
Just waiting for death to be knocking on the door.

We are the selfish ones,
We are still searching for a dream,
Which we have no more,
How their disturbed souls cry out with hunger,
There's no future for them all,
They are senseless, the earthquake-shuddered land,
And life had left them helpless,
Behind the closed eyes of the unbalanced world,
Where only Mother Earth, holds on,
To them gently close to her own breast.

*A Bhambra*

## WHEN WE ARE ONE

When the night-time comes, through the storms and rain,
When we are one, we'll be flying again.

All through the daytime, the sun and shine,
When we are one, looking out for the signs.

Looking to the heavens, through your open eyes,
When we are one, and love never dies.

When feeling all alone, through day and the night,
When we are one, you're holding me tight.

*Jamie Barnes*

## MAKE YOURSELF AT HOME

Make yourself at home
If you are already there
Enjoy the comfort
Of your old rocking chair.

Relax in the place
You love the best
Forget the jobs
Give yourself a rest.

Could you face the effort and strain
Of packing all those cases once again
Rushing off to Paris, Nice or Rome
Treat yourself and make yourself at home.

*D Sheasby*

# MY ISLAND!

Somewhere in the world
Is a land for you and me
It will be a little island
Surrounded by the sea.

The beach will be covered
In golden sand
And lots of palm trees
Shading the land.

As the sunset starts
And sky turns from blue to red,
I could sit here all day
Until I was dead.

The land of sand
And clear blue sky
A place of dreams
This is to me.

*Siobhan Charnick*

## EXMOOR

Exmoor Ponies
Tough and hardy
Graze upon green grass
Moorland beauty
Riding our bikes uphill - downhill
In Exmoor Park
Over yonder
Is the French Riviera
In our country
Lynton-by-the Sea
With its cliffs
And valleys
And
Cascading waterfalls

Wordsworth and Coleridge
And Shelley too
All wrote brilliant poetry
And brought
Even more romance
To Exmoor.

*J M Stoles*

## DAYBREAK

I am standing in the moorland
Watching little rabbits play,
Things are very peaceful here
For it is just the break of day.

My presence doesn't bother them
They are having such great fun,
But at last they spot me here
So back into the ground they run.

The little birds are singing
For they haven't got a care,
Their sounds of total happiness
Drift gently through the air.

The crows are so busy
Landing on their nest.
The screeching of the young
Must put their patience to the test.

I walk a little further on
Where fox cubs jump around.
There must be four or five
Tumbling to the ground.

The swallows glide and tumble
As flies they strive to catch,
Those things I've seen this morning
Are a lovely sight to watch.

I came here to look at sheep
My watch reads ten to seven,
I somehow get the feeling
This is a little bit like Heaven.

*Dickie Anderson*

## IN DREAMS

Have you ever wondered what it's like to fly
On wingéd Pegasus through a clear blue sky
Or to clutch a snow-white unicorn's mane
As you race the wind across an endless plain?

Can you dive with those dancers of the deep
Dolphins, in a spinning, glorious leap
And drift in the wake of majestic whales
Singing to orcas' haunting tales?

Have you ever found the end of a rainbow
And bathed in the misty, jewelled light show
Then stood in the cool silver path of the moon
As star-song echoes an ancient tune?

Have you walked in the lone, dark silent night
Feeling all around the standing stones' might
Seen visions of past lives in a crystal cave
That were spun away on the wild wind's wave?

Can you take a magical, flying carpet ride
With an enchanting genie at your side?
Will you follow a comet's swift fire-ice trail
Across velvet black space through stars' white veil?

Could you take a sword entombed in stone
Knowing it was meant for you alone?
Chant long battle sagas by a roaring fire
Then fight the man who called you a liar?

In dreams I can do all these things and more
Just close my eyes, let imagination soar
Far away from dull and ordinary days
To live in a world where dreams can blaze.

*Carolyn Fittall*

## SONG

Across the valley, the trees
Like phantoms in the mist,
Spread their shadows
Over the evening hills,
Softly, in the silence
He came without sound.
In the cool green quiet
Under the limes,
We stand close - but not touching,
Together -
Beneath a sunset sky,
Yet nothing is said
And the hours slip by.

The evening turns slowly
To silver night -
The shadowy lace of moonglow
Plays softly on his face,
And in his eyes
The hunger burns.
Those fathomless eyes -
Where teardrops dance
In widening circles
Like summer rain.

I might have cried,
For the beauty of those eyes,
But a song from long ago
Softly fills my head,
Reminding me -
How it used to be,
And is over -
Almost as soon as it's begun.

*Leonie Lewis Park*

## DREAMSCAPE

I am flying with my winged Equus
Above pale yellow clouds, I see waterfalls of nectar
Pouring from lilac mountains,
Unicorns cavort, drink from sprawling red flowers,
Their long white manes floating in a soft breeze
Filled with aromatic dreams,
I soar in wings of time, no seconds, or minutes.
Orange and green rainbows no arcs across the sky,
Straight lines on the horizon. It is pleasant here.

Your dark eyes, sweet pools of treacle diaphanous against a pink sea,
I sense you, delicate butterfly wings breeze within me,
I hear your silent words; I close my eyes, pour myself into you
Liquids of velvet mingle,
I drown in our intensity, our nakedness shameless
In slow motion we float as one
Gliding over mirrored lakes reflecting our love each to the other,
Bitter-sweet from its conception strong and true in its fruition,
Forbidden fruit in wakefulness, in dreams always tastes sweetest.

Mortals in awe of love that strengthens with separation,
Puzzled by the uniting of souls, Twin Ka's on an astral plane,
Two hearts that will always beat together
But are fated by melancholic destiny to be apart.
Love closeted in shadows but forged on lightning's bolt,
Branded on the living, broken hearts of ill-fated lovers.
In our dreamscape, we can walk the threshold of light,
Ignore the hands that tick-tock time, no fingers of accusation
Nor tongues of barbed prose will harm us,
Only the pain in the realms that change night into day.

*Helen Posgate*

## COBBLED SHORES OF BALINTORE

Come with me, and share some time
On the shores of Balintore
It's so unspoiled and natural
Just one big rocky shore

I've gone there since my younger days
And quieter, it all seems
It's somewhere you could walk for miles
To think, or just to dream

You have the best of summer's dreams
For just a wee bit along the shore
It's then you come to Shandwick
And golden sands galore

There are a few new houses
With little there to do
But there's plenty of peace and tranquillity
A writer's dream come true

Not many come to use the beach
Like it was once before
I can remember lots of children
Playing on the sunny shore

But the village, it really didn't grow that much
And the jobs there aren't any
The fishing boats they are so few
For to earn an extra penny

But if you ever care to visit
There is one thing sure you'll find
Pure air, fresh winds, and solitude
The perfect tonic for your mind.

*Florrie MacGruer*

## A DREAM AND REALITY

I do not want to fly on Concorde
Or take a trip to the moon.
But a gentle ride in a basket
Of a colourful hot air balloon.

To drift over fields and hilltops
The quiet valleys below.
Away from the bustle and bus stops
Enjoying the air's gentle flow.

Quietness, peace and respite
A calm and tranquil ride.
The soul refreshed and set alight
To face once more the flow and tide.

This may be a dream, but I can go
On a quiet journey each day.
When I ask the One who pilots my life
To guide me another day.

*F L Brain*

## RIVER LANDSCAPE BY A LITTLE-KNOWN ARTIST

Where does this path lead? The dark river gleams
Reflecting trees and hills and clouds and sky,
Stirred only by the splash of falling streams
And a bird's dripping wings swift-skimming by.

The path is shaded by majestic trees
Below the mountainside where thick firs grow,
Their scent blown downward by a gentle breeze
Fresh from the regions of eternal snow.

To wander on forever through this glade,
The slowly-moving water winding still
Down wondrous valleys under sun and shade
Of misty silver clouds that crown the hill;

To wander here forever is a dream;
Vision - like midnight glimpses shadowy white,
Faint moonlit peaks, pale lake, and shimmering stream,
Or sunrise over low mist filled with light.

For this is but a picture, painted so;
Though we can feel the air that fans the pool,
Breathe the clean wind from unseen heights of snow
Along the river pathway, sweet and cool.

O unknown painter what great art was yours
To make so true this place of light and shade;
These clouded mountains and the purple moors,
The dark fir forest and green high-branched glade.

Out of the colour of the earth and sky
Mysterious landscape leading far away,
Water forever flowing slowly by,
What gift from heaven to paint eternal day.

*Diana Momber*

## SHELTERED OASIS

My dream is a place
of a quiet oasis,
to ponder and think awhile.
To relax and sit
for a little bit,
for speed is not my style.

I could study the beauty of nature,
with all its magnificent hues,
and could look at many pathways
and decide which one to choose.

To be thankful for many gifts,
and hum cheerily as I walk,
and maybe with a wonderful friend,
be silent or perhaps talk.

A little stroll, a panoramic scene,
what bliss and joy it would really mean.
Some animals in a field quietly grazing,
and me on the grass happily lazing!

*Gloria S Beeston*

## MY FARAWAY SHORE

My place of dreams is far away
In the Emerald Isle,
The people are so friendly
On their face you'll always see a smile.

Every time I go there,
I am over-awed,
By the forty shades of green
And the rivers that unfold.

Then there's the sleepy shores
You can walk along at ease,
Sorting out one's problems
On your face, the blowing of a breeze.

The mountains looming high above,
Above the valleys down below.
You'll only hear the birds sing
As the peaceful waters flow.

The sheep and lambs are grazing
In the fields at early spring.
On a Sunday morning the church bells
                              you'll hear ring.

There are so many small islands
Uninhabited now are they,
I wonder what life was like,
In many a bygone day.

Yes, folk, my place of dreams
Is that of a Donegal shore,
You only have to go there once
And in your heart it'll remain forever more.

*Yvonne Lewis*

## SOUTH STACK

A past has returned to haunt my tomorrows,
I must step back, to a time of childhood days, once more,
to see the steep drop of your craggy cliffs,
embellished by fleawort and thrift,
where oystercatchers stop by,
where guillemots and tern swoop down to poise upon your
warning beacon, bethroned in the Irish Sea.

Too soon nimbus clouds gather.
I watch, as a foalhardy fishing boat,
with lanterns swinging at the prow, awaits
to haul its catch;
then, sensing danger from a freshening breeze,
seeks refuge from dark passages of gloomy
awesome caves.

A red sun, descends into the horizon of a lucent sea,
waiting to rise, in yet another day;
when artists, twitchers, and the like,
will come to sketch and snapshots take,
of your august majesty.

South Stack, you haunt my every day with bygone memories.
Long since gone the old familiar faces,
that graced your shores in halcyon days.
Replaced by geological day trippers
chipping, at your soul.

I shall come to you, one day at twilight,
when darkened hours are few,
and linger, in approving silence of the day's end,
only then, as I breathe the salty air of Holy Island,
will my nostalgia be satisfied.

*Margaret Frow*

## TENNYSON DOWN

Strange how my thoughts return, homing again,
Like birds to the nest when the greyness of evening falls
Over the silent earth, for the soul's core too
Has twilights of greyness. Home, then, the spirit sweeps,
Home to the heaven-haven, island of peace,
Winging in fancy over the sea-blanched cliffs,
Over the wind-cropped grass where the purple flower
Clings to precarious life and the lone gull soars,
Circling and screaming over the naked shore,
And the small white boats sail on through the purple sea.

*Jackie Lapidge*

## DREAM-KEEPER

Seen out of its protective shell,
it can cause people to scream.
It is supposed to be protected,
to prevent it becoming infected.
Incredibly delicate and sensitive,
emotional, creative and inventive.

To keep the dream-keeper active,
don't allow it to become inactive.
Use it frequently, whenever possible,
ask it to do what seems impossible.

Keep it well, feed it with information,
don't treat it, with careless denigration.
Because the wrinkly grey matter,
capable of making people scream.
is the safest place, to keep a dream.

*Mandy Ann Cole*

## MOUNTAIN BOTTOM

Mountain bottom, that's where I want to retire,
watch climbers and skiers, in front of my fire.
Occasionally walk, to the summit of cloud,
feel fit at sixty-five, and oh! so very proud.
For actually having achieved a lifelong dream,
one which, when aged forty, began to seem
Almost impossible, a flightful fantasy of mind,
but now I've left my old negativity behind.
Dreams are useful, they keep me alive,
they are sustenance, on which I thrive.

And now, when I have time to pass,
I dream of lush, short green grass.
In my garden, at the bottom of a slope,
my home in reality, one day I hope.

Deckchair, when warm, log fire when colder,
and, inevitably, a ski lift for when I'm older!

*Danny Coleman*

## ANCIENT WISDOMS

Singing winds and whispering waters; laughing rills and silent meres;
lonely clouds and rain-clad sunlight; aching hearts and human fears . . .
Everflowing rivers running; runic symbols fill my eyes;
pain too deep for mortal telling dwells forever with the wise.

Ancient words their spells a-casting, signs and wonders to perform;
faerie green, and slow enchantment, melt the sun and still the storm.
Magic worlds and grave-cold oceans; minds quiet-haunted
                                                    by their fears;
time and life imbued with sorrow; cries of pain that no one hears.

Grail of myth, and knights of legend; sea-green halls in castles lost;
snow-capped mountains, ice-cold senses; peaceful dreams by
                                                    nightmares tossed . . .
Starry realms and scarlet wishes; robes of gold, embroidered moons;
white-edged thought, all power given, with the casting of the runes . . .

Spinning seas and rivers dancing; ancient symbols newly drawn;
joy and tears, all life enhancing, fill the eyes and heart at dawn.
Words and wand mark out the circle; hold the stars and clutch
                                                    the sun . . .
Dream the dream, and wish the thought form - grasp the skies,
                                                    the deed is done.

Fiery winds and earth-cooled waters; singing rills and quiet meres;
storm-charged clouds and sky-clad sunlight; crying hearts, and
                                                    moon-washed tears.
Earth and Air, and Fire and Water . . . Golden dreams that haunt
                                                    the mind . . .
Pain, beyond all mortal telling - dwell forever with the wise . . .

*Jenny Proom*

## HAPPINESS IS A STATE OF MIND

My place of dreams is peace of mind, a place where all are
thoughtful and kind.
My place of dreams is where people care, and are never spiteful
and unfair.

My place of dreams is a place where harsh words are never spoken,
and past hurts are never woken.
My place of dreams is where smiles and laughter are never
used to shame,
Where mockery is never used to apportion blame.

This is the dream to which I had always aspired,
My story now has a happy end with freedom and the love and support
of friends,
My place of dreams I have now acquired.

*Brenda Rollo*

## BOAYL ARD GHOOGHYSSAGHT (ELLAN VANNIN)

Summer winds of friendly Manx conversation, govern in
ancient ways,
an island where people live their dreams, and dream their days.
Winds of Celtic history kiss lips
and service storytelling seagulls' quips.

In the breezes of childhood memories, that gently sway the gorse,
a million fuchsia blooms devote impassioned applause.
Harbour lights tell fishing tales to passing solicitudes
and waters of the evening, lyrically lap the province in preludes.

Immodest headlands peak above under-clouds,
clothed in purple silken heather, proud.
While wildlife covets tame-life and scripts torrid yarns in bedrock,
moonlight paints candlelight, into discreet valleys of
wild garlic and hock.
Softened lush-dawn joyfulness awakens boggit-terrain
under Loaghtan hooves,
close to blushing homestead cottages, thatched with
Sunday cassag-roofs.

Gushing streams fill glens with precious adornment
While Little Ones perform precocious entertainment
Under the cloak of Mannanan,
the secret of Man kisses the beauty of woman.
An ancient sun returns from history, to warm parts intimate

And as beauty and history consummate,
Immortal Isle of Man, that passion! Perpetuation!
- that which defies any mortal, not to feel infatuation.

*Adrian Trowbridge*

## CUBA
*(Dedico ésta poema a mis compadres*
*Cubanos - en particular Vladamir)*

I feel like an alien in my own town
Life here is never going to be the same
Now that I've fallen in love
With hot, dirty, crazy Havana.

The days blurred into one,
The nights were endless
The laughter incessant
The band with Havaneros unbreakable.

I loved the danger -
being stopped by police because
we hung around with Cubanos.

I loved being stuck in a Russian-style hotel
lift in Santa Maria del Mar -
knowing the warm turquoise waves
were waiting for me outside.

I loved eating black beans and rice
by candlelight,
watching my new friends using
cigarette lights to see their meals,
used to the regular powercuts.

I loved taking the rickety ferry boat
over the harbour of Havana
and standing by the statue of Christ,
overlooking my wonderful new home.

I dream about Cuba every night
I wish I hadn't left my heart and soul there.

*Anon*

## DREAMLAND

I lie in my bed, I drift off to sleep
And into Dreamland I take a peep.
I weave and tumble my dreams aloft
The bed is comfy, the pillow soft.

I dream of Andy, my kind, sweet nurse
Always a pleasure never a curse.
I dream of our sessions of talking things out
Of his permanent care I'm never in doubt.

We talk about many things indeed
To my words he does pay heed.
It's like being upon a fluffy cloud
He's always quiet, never loud.

And from my dream I wake in peace
For I know in reality his care will not cease.
He is my nurse that I love so much
And in my dream we get in touch.

*Denise Shaw*

## A DREAM

I walked on the Heath where the foxgloves grow
  In delicate light by the stream,
And high in the fields where the grasses blow
  And I picked myself a dream.

The dream that I picked from among the flowers,
  The dream that swung soft in the breeze,
That dream was of golden and sun-warmed hours,
  And was full of ecstasies.

And oh my darling, my dearest one,
  My love, 'twas a sweet dream of you,
I woke from my dream in the golden sun
  And I knew I'd a dream come true.

*G Poole*

## MY FAVOURITE PLACE

Sometimes I need to get away
to my dream place
far away,
Just me and my dog
on a sandy shore
Away from the noise
and traffic roar,
Where I can swim,
or read a book
Someone else can shop and cook
So I close my eyes
and I'm on that beach
out of everybody's reach
feel the warm sun upon my face
This is just my favourite place.

*Susan Davies*

## MY DREAM

Walk the sloping narrow road, wild flower flanked
Towards the sea, seagulls mewling overhead
Sun shines from brilliant blue, fluffy white cloud banked
The sea blue-green, echoes of the Med
To the left, wild, wild heather-strewn moor
The right a cottage, thatched, roses round the door
All is peace, waves lapping gently on the shore
A far, far cry from its thunderous winter roar
Walk on burning sand, towards inviting sea
Damp sand where tide had ebbed, panders to my feet
Lonely tranquil beach, with no one there but me
With tentative step, the cooling waters meet
Time to sit alone, to ponder on life's path
Time to dream my dreams, make some exciting plan
This is my silent dream, with no harsh aftermath
Bask alone in pleasant sun and get a tan.

*Dora Watkins*

## MY DREAM ISLAND

Many a night I have dreamt of this beautiful island
With its shores of glittering golden sands
The sea adorned with its ravishing scent

Trees of magnificent stature circle the shoreline
They give shelter from the sun
Each one green, luscious and of mighty height
Like an everlasting umbrella

The peace of my island tells its own story
Only the gentle lapping of the waves are ever heard
But in the sea activity is abounding

A school of dolphins can be seen basking
Offshore, watching my every move
They seem to call me in their fish language
I am tempted to go to them, I have known the enjoyment before

Swimming leisurely towards them
And when the sea is deep enough for them to come to me
We play together happily until I'm tired

Before I fall asleep the dolphins
Push me towards the seashore
I find myself at dawn
Awake from the sleep, the dolphins are gone

Delicious food seems to appear from nowhere
And always my special variety
I eat it ravishingly

To enjoy a walk in the shade of the beautiful trees
I wander along full of awe
At the sight I behold
Then, I am back in my bed to awaken to the morning dew.

*Alma Montgomery Frank*

# NIGHT

The moon upon the water shines,
And stars like fireflies
Are mirrored in the sea,
Then the rhythm of the waves
Brings peace again to me.

As darkness folds in like a balm
Forming a blanket,
Warm and comforting,
Hiding all that does not please
And things that take away my ease.

The everlasting motion of the sea,
Its music as it crashes
On the shore,
Then quietly recedes
To come again once more.

Then shapes of ships upon the shore,
And those that glide upon the sea,
Faint shapes like phantoms
In the dark,
Symbols of the days of yore.

So the peace of night
Wafts gently on the breeze,
And lets us dream of unknown things
While looking at the universe,
At night beside the sea.

Then dawn throws out her fingertip,
And streams across the sky,
Searching out the shadows
And destroying one by one,
Ready to start a brand new day.

*Joan May Wills*

# AUTUMN DAYS

Silver birch trees standing tall,
clothed with the golden leaves of Fall;
stirring gently and glowing with faerie light,
shimmering, ethereal and bright.

Against the backdrop of majestic hills
the lake before them gently spills
its lapping waters, fed from streams above,
whilst shadows in the sunlight move.

All is warm and calm and still,
till music breaks forth from beak and bill;
bird and water, hill and tree
speak of the Creator's majesty.

Man and all of creation, at one in peace,
bound in harmony that has never ceased
from the beginning of time, to these days,
each offering a thankful song of praise.

*Catherine Riley*

# 'TO SEE OLD TINTERN ABBEY RIGHT, PLEASE VISIT IT BY PALE MOONLIGHT'

One evening I went to wander about the picturesque, impressive, stately
atmospheric ruins of a Cistercian Abbey in a peaceful valley,
perfectly set at foot of a deep limestone gorge, in a loop by
                                                    'Sylvan Wye',
shining silver torque in a green-lined case, its wooded hills and
grassy meadow vistas framed by elegant, delicate, empty ancient
                                                    tracery.
I was intrigued, enchanted by the sublime antiquity and mystery
of this aesthetic pilgrimage place. Even after centuries of desolation
and decay, these grey, sombre, simple outlines had magnificent power,
splendid grandeur to stir the soul, yet a certain modesty.

Before nightfall, the weather calm, quiet, the great building glowed,
Tintern's walls were warm as those of rose-tinted Petra.
While the light faded, I roamed among majestic pillars and arches,
entered doorways, fine Decorated, through one via the outer parlour:
salutary to reflect that a medieval visitor got no further.

After sunset, mist filled, a curtain veiled the valley,
through which shimmered the Abbey, tenuous, insubstantial.
Come darkness, dewfall; the moon arose, its light slowly grew,
silver against deep indigo, owls hooted across woods, 'oohoo, oohoo.'
Alone, I heard not a whisper, watched sharp shadows
creep into smooth turfed aisles, transepts emerge as
transformed objects from self-created shapes of blackness.

Later yet, the church stood silver-swathed, still as the bones of those
who lay beneath - canons, priests, deacons, laymen, white-robed friars,
all in their way once swelled the universal hymn of praise.
No illuminated letter, scripture phrase, song of choirs, chord of music
was ever tinted, better turned, sweeter sung, finer tuned
than that imperfect, perfect ruin, bathed in moonlight,
but no past divine tintinnabulation or chanted devotion
ruffled the last peace of those vast crumbled walls at Tintern.

*David Daymond*

## Our Thoughts In Harmony

In life's motion you see a far distant pool,
Hear murmuring waters, serene and cool,
An urge to follow that meandering stream,
Not an illusion, but a beckoning dream.

In life's repose, be as a mirror dark yet clear,
See images of loved ones, near and dear.
Stifle fears and doubts seen in the dark,
Let thoughts fly free as a soaring lark.

Be quiet as a recurring echo, far yet so near,
'Darling I see you but cannot hear'
Speak no words that hurt a troubled mind,
Judge not, no barbs, be subtle, be kind.

Through our lives, all motions will be as waters still,
Whilst in repose, let all emotions thrill,
In thought and deed, be an echo clear,
Be calm, be subtle to those who wish to hear.

*K Aukett*

## RIDING ON A CLOUD

Riding on a cloud,
She sings.
Fortress forcing passage on.
Words are futile, dreams are real.
Bracing winds she dares to steal.

All the madness
Drives below,
Firmament like danger's kill.
She finds pace, she laughs at how
Solving air clues must allow.

Weather's put away,
No sail.
Bring it back, that deity dare.
Treading rain, some pressure hold,
Riding clouds, her brow is cold.

If, beleaguered friends,
You look,
Gull-winged ships are full of hope.
Riding lofted nimbus chain,
Hers the fortune needs retain.

Press-ganged fleet on
Reddened sky,
Cloak of sun lost to the eve.
She, that passenger, bold of scent;
She, that vessel, crossing spent.

*S Pete Robson*

## ARE YOU DREAMING?

Building castles in the air
Cement your imaginations
Build your rocky emotions
Yet, don't throw your hands in the air
Out of tranquillity, an outburst
To build a city in days the worst
Make known your ambition and hear
'Friend, are you dreaming?'
Daydream on what never was
Weave on the fibre yet to come
In the realms of the mind
'When you've closed your eyes'
Remembering last night
When he committed adultery
With eyes shut, 'I love you'
Wife demanding, 'Are you dreaming?'
Into battle with a cut throat
In the heat of the Sahara, deserted
Browse the area for an oasis
Screen: Access denied
Today's dream seeks a scream
Eyes shut, he's about to cut
Don't heed, open your eyes
'Are you dreaming?'
An old witch is encountered
Tells him, he'll die tomorrow
Over a barrier of imagination
From a nobody to a somebody
Even if contrary, hear him say
'Are you dreaming?'

*Ato Ulzen-Appiah*

## SOLITUDE

When the world around starts to worry me
And my troubles are too great,
I like to leave them all behind
And sit and meditate.

When the noise of the traffic is roaring
And I'm getting to my wits' end,
I like to go to a quiet place
With God as my only friend.

Alone with God and with nature,
My vows to him renewed,
All my cares are left behind me
As I rest in solitude.

*Joyce Walker*

## JOURNEY OF DREAMS

I'm looking to the heavens in a mansion white that's there
To a room that's filled with thoughts where decisions are
                                                judged and fair
There I see two rows of people twelve on either side
Of a man sat in the centre with his hands on eyes to hide
The grief of what he's seeing in a ball of crystal blue
Is the hurt of all humanity showing through the hue
In tears he stands and turns his head to summon his servant bold
Prepare a ship for travel to a world where care's gone cold
So out he walks on marble black a whole departure pad
To leave the ones whose shining clear minds that cure bad
True waves wish him well in being ideas in guided flight
Of extended hearts in knowing He'll be steered by the light
Of a million stars in journey cross a spiritual heavenly place
Where his hand commands the wheel and starts to turn the human race
Round mountains high in ego to silver fountains spraying gold
To show the earth is open to love to have to hold
Its memories of eternity and peace, approaching silent from above
To land this graceful father safe on this test that's meant with love.

*W Pooley*

## HAGA HAGA BEACH, SOUTH AFRICA

Shredded sunlight sifting on honey-gold sand,
Halcyon pools, rock-rimmed, topaz-tanned,
Wind plume, spray spume
From the crinkled, silvering sea.

Sunlight, eye-bright, highlight, skylight,
Clouds pearl, unfurl, eddies swirl, clouds pearl,
Above the wrinkled, whispering sea.

Wave-beat, heartbeat, minute traces
Of minuscule feet -
Snail trail, crab claw,
Opaline shells scatter the shore -
Waves break, heartache, angelfish, sea snake,
Horseshoe beach, green-feathered strand,
Seagulls scour the glistening land.

*Jane Finlayson*

## FORCE OF GRAVITY

As we watched the shapes appear,
Clouds like rising land,
Seas and shores above yet near,
Bright golden was the sand.

High mountains of granite grey,
Seemed solid as truth,
Yet broke, drifted all away,
Of firmness left no proof.

Lands of smoke and mist and cloud,
From our imagination,
Vivid impression which allowed,
Hope of visitation.

To walk that ethereal hill,
Welcomed at some hall,
Yet, one thought destroyed the thrill,
We might fall through it all!

*Kathleen M Scatchard*

## DUNGEON DREAMS

Can I get solitary confinement
Without actually committing a crime?
Can I pick a cell as my apartment.
I want peace and quiet. I need the time
Away from loud people, free from the crowd.
I'm a lot less lonely all on my own.
I know I shouldn't really be allowed
In when most inmates want out and they moan
That they won't come back, but most of them do
While I'm punished for being innocent.
What if I break a window? Would that do
For at least short-term prison internment?
I'm an atheist so the monastery
Won't take me in and look after me.

*Arthur Chappell*

## ABOVE THE SUN

Sleeping in a temple,
Subconscious on the run,
Drift and we will meet you,
Far above the sun.

Yellow crashes amber,
We need no word at al,1
Warmer to the lining,
So touch us one and all.

Close your eyes and follow,
The blinding light of me,
Watching as we're waiting,
The feeling that we're free.

Flying on reflection,
Shot through a coloured gun,
Asking can we stay here,
Far above the sun.

*Lee Severns*

## DREAMING

I dreamed I was in a far-off land
I thought I was in Paradise
Rolling waves and golden sand
'Neath beautiful azure skies

Days of lying in the sun
With not a single care
It's as if my life has just begun
The answer to my prayer

I dreamed I saw a handsome man
Strolling on the shore
Eyes of blue and a golden tan
Who could ask for more?

He came and took me by the hand
To show me wonders new
The beauty of this foreign land
Was all this really true?

Slowly, gently, I awake
If only I could stay
But now it's time to make the break
Then dream again another day.

*Grace Wallace*

# GARDEN HOUSE

We walked towards the garden house
The walls a lilac hue
Wisteria curling up the walls
Disappearing out of view

Here the garden of my dreams
Starts its wending path
Around so many changing scenes
The eye to surely cast

Wander through the Acers
In their different coloured robes
In graceful folds of shady leaves
They hang in silent mode

Azaleas in pink and gold
Heavy in scented bloom
Mixed with rhododendrons
Above your head they loom

You'll find a high-walled garden
With secrets to unfold
A summer house to rest a while
Its thatch now grey and old

Sit a while your eyes half-closed
The birds you'll hear in song
The fragrance of the blossoms
Drifting past, then gone

So much to see but time to go
From this garden house of dreams
Though in your mind you'll always keep
All wonders heard and seen.

***Beryl Smyter***

## MORECAMBE BAY

So! 'Twas here I was placed
Where life's beauty surrounds
Part of my town's motto
Includes 'And health abounds'
Nowhere else could you find
Such a wondrous sight
My sunsets are magic
And capture those nights
I take in two local rivers
And the Irish Sea
They help create its harmony
When people say 'Nothing in life is free'
It is plain they haven't yet
Cast their eyes upon me!
One's views are stunning
On a fine, clear day.
And it is all down to nature
Who made me this way.
My setting is perfect
It fills me with pride
You can also walk across me
With a guide at certain tides.

*Joyce M Hargreaves*

## MAGIC CARPET RIDE

Sitting on a plush carpet swirling and swinging and taking me
Seeing things that weren't there.
A tree, a bush, a chair
Rain in my hair
Planes fly by, birds in the tree
Rainbows and clouds and waves in the sea.
Thunder and hailstones are a thing of the past
Believe me.
I'm sailing like a yacht in a race
With wind blowing so softly in my face
No more passports, no more fares
A free carpet ride to the sea.
Islands of green, seas of blue, coconuts
Paradise and bananas too.
Animals look and stare seeing so high up
Toiling in the air.
Holding on tight all through the night
Sleeping on dreamily, oh what a ball.
Seeing me with Aladdin, it's like a fairy tale come true
Full of hope, happiness and love too.
Houses so tall the buildings whoops the wall
It's hard to keep still, the excitement, the thrill
It's like a speedboat on a lake,
A duck or even a drake.
Crushing of heartbeats, closing of eyes
Hoping and praying will be alright.
All I was doing was reading a tale.
A prince with a girl whom he loved.
Very much and the rest I was flying
                    away on it with lush.

*A J Renyard*

## SUCCESS

People say I'm different
And somehow I think I am
For my dreams don't extend to
Cruising with the rich man in a faraway land
My dreams are not for me
They are for the less fortunate than me
For I have already mingled with the famous
And gee, what a time that was!
My only dreams now are for the children of today
I wish for their pain to go away
I wish for a mentor to guide them every day
And steer them clear of life's troublesome path
And make their lives successful in every way
So one day they'll reach their paradise
That special place they dream of day after day.

*Carolie Pemberton*

## THE HOLLOW

Come with me to a house of joy
Perched high upon the hill,
The day is fair as I set off
For a picnic with the Lord.
Down the driveway, round the bush
Blooming with vibrant colour.
Up the rugged path I go, the Crags so close at hand.
The trees are singing in the breeze
The grass joins in as well.
Over the style, into the fields
The sheep they scatter everywhere.
I find the little hollow and gladly settle in.
I gaze in awesome wonder at the work of Father's hand.
The trees, the fields, the river, the rugged stony crags.
We spend the day so quietly in love, in joy and peace,
A little haven of perfect peace in the presence of my Lord.
And then it suddenly struck me 'twas no hollow in the land,
For the place that I was sitting, was the hollow of God's hand.

*Nessie Shaw*

## MY LOVE

A place
Where?
A dream
Where?
If I do look
If I do trust
Where?
Where?
On the wings of the bird soaring high in the sky.
My dream will fly.
In my thoughts of the one I love.

*Anne MacLeod*

## DREAMING

When I was young some of the things I read would send me
                                          into a dream,
But was told not to be silly as most would be unlikely to be seen.
As I grew older that was to change,
I belonged to a travel club and therefore had most of my
                                          holidays arranged.
My work was in a very busy place,
So quiet times I could always face.
Sometimes it was abroad - others, we stayed home,
But wherever we went we found places to roam.
We would lose ourselves for a few days
Sampling many new and intricate ways
Where there was plenty of water one saw the bright colours
                                          of a rainbow
Or perhaps see glorious sunsets all aglow.
See snow lying very thickly in July,
As we passed foreign townships by.
Drink in the peace and quiet of a lovely scene,
The memory of which will always help you to stay serene.
At home amble through a quiet wood,
And your dreaming is bound to help you do some good.

*Betty Green*

## STORM CLOUDS OVER BURRY HOLM

I read tales of drowning and other dreadful deaths
on the tombs in the picturesque churchyard
but some were too old to decipher
with no flowers placed there for many a year.
The sun broke through turning the hills gold,
shining on the perilously perched sheep
and the wreck of the Helvetia with just
an accusing finger jutting from the sea.

Later, the weather turned and Worm's Head
was encased with a celestial glow
but storm clouds obscured Burry Holm
where violent waves competed with each other,
trying to reach the summit of that bleak place
as I shivered from the rain, cold
and the wind which blew the city from my soul.

Today there was only my footprints on the sand
and I felt like an explorer in an undiscovered land
as I listened to the snarl of the untamed sea
and watched the foam which was like soft snow
chase each other like lambs at play.
The distance was deceptive, I trudged on
and finally reached this mystical scene
as thunder roared and hail slammed against my face
but this was freedom under a darkened dome
with the wailing wind and wild waves of Burry Holm.

*Guy Fletcher*

## SUNRISE

and the flickering, snickering hues
lure the avid eye,
toy with the coy avoidance
of a cloud's vulvar mimicry.

Indescribable waves of shades
roll towards an azure beach
littered with surreal bladderwrack.

Then an immense mint penny
glints distantly,
a hopeful epigram;
beacon of potential.

Someone nearby sighs and,
for a moment,
I am puzzled -
being alone.

***Perry McDaid***

## COMING HOME (HEAVEN)

I kissed the world goodbye
And through the mists of time an angel called my name
A faultless peace unto me came
I am where eagles cannot fly
Beyond a bright and cloudless sky
Completeness now is mine
For I am held in perfect love divine
The bonds of earth that weighed me down
Are broken now with sacred love
Swathed in beauty, harmony and rest
My campaign won. I am not lost
With Him who died upon that cross.

*Shirley Webster*

# SUBMISSIONS INVITED
## *SOMETHING FOR EVERYONE*

**POETRY NOW 2001** - Any subject,
any style, any time.

**WOMENSWORDS 2001** - Strictly women,
have your say the female way!

**STRONGWORDS 2001** - Warning!
Age restriction, must be between 16-24,
opinionated and have strong views.
(Not for the faint-hearted)

All poems no longer than 30 lines.
Always welcome! No fee!
Cash Prizes to be won!

Mark your envelope (eg *Poetry Now*) **2001**
Send to:
Forward Press Ltd
Remus House, Coltsfoot Drive,
Peterborough, PE2 9JX

## OVER £10,000 POETRY PRIZES
## TO BE WON!

Judging will take place in October 2001